We *Live* and *Learn*

"At a Life Pace"

CLAUDIA WALTHING ANDRADE

We Live and Learn

Copyright © 2021 by Claudia Walthing Andrade. All rights reserved.

No part of this publication may be reproduced, stored in a retrieval system or transmitted in any way by any means, electronic, mechanical, photocopy, recording or otherwise without the prior permission of the author except as provided by USA copyright law.

The opinions expressed by the author are not necessarily those of URLink Print and Media.

1603 Capitol Ave., Suite 310 Cheyenne, Wyoming USA 82001
1-888-980-6523 | admin@urlinkpublishing.com

URLink Print and Media is committed to excellence in the publishing industry.

Book design copyright © 2021 by URLink Print and Media. All rights reserved.

Published in the United States of America

Library of Congress Control Number: 2020915687
ISBN 978-1-64753-466-0 (Paperback)
ISBN 978-1-64753-467-7 (Digital)

30.07.20

Dedication

I DEDICATE THIS BOOK TO MY LORD, HIS HOLY SON JESUS, and TO MY SUPPORTIVE SON JESUS WALTHING CURIEL JR.

"Let the beauty of the father of father's be upon us and establish the work of our hands for us. Yes, establish the work of our hands."

—Psalm 90:17

Family

Mother

My mother is wonderful
With a beautiful smile
God made her to be my mother
She's like no other
Her name is Maria
She named me Claudia
Mothers' love is like
A free kite you see up in the sky
As a strong single mother
She cared for four children
Me, Ezequiel, Laurie, and Cesar
She also had other four grown
That she nurtured with our father

We were always protected
From harm with care by mother
Taught us to always have respect
Just like a protective mother bear
Her advices & traits I started to collect.
She protects her cubs with care
Her defenses are her sharp teeth
Defending her offspring from danger
At night watching us when we breathe

Mother bear's claws are hard & strong
Yes, mother raised us with the support
Of my fourth older brother Sergio
I absolutely, love our mother gave us comfort
She's the greatest anyone can ever know
As I got older, I once told her
I was going to be like her & more
My mother is a happy and lovable
Individual talks to everyone she meets

With a sweet smile that is likeable
Holding up with her kindhearted
As a child she's been my role model
She has always been energetic
Seven years ago, I was Epileptic
My delightful mom raised us four
Even though we had to share
Her affection, attention, and her
Forever love between us four
We ate delicious meals never slept
On bare cold floor or dirt
Watched our growth every step
From vaccinations to outgrown shirt
Mother did what she could to raise us
It's our turn to give her love & more
More than, she ever gave us before & embrace
The plenty of love she keeps us together

Mother use to work from dawn to sunset
I never got to see or heard any regrets
As she came home exhausted and late
Mother came home from her first job
She worked hard under the burning sun
Never saw her worried or heard her sob
In her evening job she was a cook
She knew the menu like a memorized book
Mother's co-workers called her "Cookie",
For the fact she has a sweet smile,
Full of energy, cheerful and warming
Willing to go that extra mile
Mother was not afraid to work
We were not rich or even poor
On her birthday we see fireworks
We're always content around her
We never asked her for more
None the less, what she could afford
Her strong will managed her
To pull us through and still hold
With her sweat on her forehead
Adding to her honest work
She thanked God for our daily bread
We all love the way she still cooks

She covered her daily stress
Behind her warm & caring look
Underneath that wrinkle dress
Through life I read her like a book
My mother is extraordinarily strong hearted lady
I thank God for giving her to me
To appreciate and love every day
Take a deep look at me & you'll see
I will always be there for her any day

Never knew exactly where mother
I believe she got help from our brother
We needed new pair of shoes
Me & my three youngest siblings
She bought us a nice pair of shoes
So, we can wear to our first day school
I honestly love my dear mother
My friends then and now say she's cool
I'm proud of mother for her scarifies
In raising us with her enormous heart
Now each of us has our own different lives
Raising our own family and doing our task
She's always in my thoughts but never apart
From my son's & my heart to my prayer at night

You can see why I wrote this poem about her
Between paper & words you have met my mother.

"She is clothed with strength and dignity; she can laugh at days to come."
-Proverbs 31:25

Significant Faded Photograph

After forty-two years I finally meet you
Your unique & familiar image I embrace
I see your face on my father & on my nephew
I see your dusty eyes on my father's eyes
I was determined to have a picture of you
My determination was strong & not like those
That comes to a dead end and don't know
Their family's roots not knowing they have clues
I inherited your creativity with wood like you
My father's light skin color is like yours
I heard by my mother you were a workaholic, too
A significant photograph is more than a heritage
You had the charm for the ladies like Romeo
Without your photograph my heart was confuse
To obtain this fading picture was my, peruse
Father told me to forget about it more than ones
He never saw my reason & point of view about you
To have your last name I never want to lose
I wish I had the chance to know you long ago
To know about you and this picture was a chance
I'm proud to hold your last name on my blood flow
I no longer carry my heart with an empty space
I wish I could tell you what I had to go through
To find about you & holding this picture was good news
I show your picture off to those don't know about you
Like to my siblings, close friends, nieces & nephews
Father looks so much like you and it really shows

Father not being your son it's something he can't refuse
He gained your charm with the ladies from head to toe
To know more family members & about you is my focus
Your significant fading photograph I always knew
I would have someday & now you're in a special place
In my heart & became someone I can easily lean-to
Your fading photograph puts a smile on my face
I don't mind how many hoops I have to go through
To gather as much information in my memory case
So, I can share with the coming future, too
To cherish memories for many coming days
My enjoyment meeting you makes my face glow.

I love you Grandpa Ernesto Walting!

"Gray hair is a crown of glory; it is gained a righteous life."

-Proverbs 16:31

Heart of the Family

This hard and especially workaholic mother straight
Will proudly say she gave birth to fifteen
Carrying a burden of seven ceased & nurtured eight
Survived she became full time mother as a young teen.
They all came from the same bloodline of parents
At dinner time I was the fifth plate never had to wait
For being the fifth child, I was never served late
To passed down clothing we never hesitated
Mother's love for us as kids was never a transient
Because now as grown adults she still demonstrates
Her love for us it's hard for her to see we don't
Communicate like before because life treated
Each of us harder than one another but it's not late
To come together for mother regardless our estate
There's no mother that can be a double or replicate.
Thanks to the heart of the family each
Of us have different traits to our kids we need to teach.
Not hold grudges from each other & be compassionate
If we just forget about the past and cooperate
Just to see mother smile that would be a memorable date
Let's go back to the childhood memories & recapitulate
You will see that by looking back it's not a profligate
Time it will not make you better but more sapient
Yes, we disagree & say hurtful things even prate
Especially when our minds are mix-up under a stimulate
That's their way of asking to help them to bring

Them home away from the demons with substantiate
The heart is strong and yet so sensitive and delicate
To see her children are growing apart she learned to tolerate
It's time for her children to recapture and reactivate
The moments of closeness and do things she taught
Her children to stay together and appreciate
The most valuable anyone can ever have to say good night

Today because tomorrow it may be lost forever parent.

*I dedicate this worthy writing to those that are going through hard time dealing with not being close to family like before. And to those who simply care for others who have the same blood running through their veins; like no others around you. Happiness is those you grew up with and played together even shared the same bed as kids. You may be even that person who your sibling looked up to at one point in life as growing up. Most of all I created this for my loving brothers and sister and most of all for the woman who gave us life and nurture us through the toughest storms. Yes, I am talking about our mother so let's keep the smile on her face.

"Honor your father and mother, that your days may be long in the land that the Lord your God is giving you."
-Exodus 20:12

My Very Own Miracle

He was born premature baby and so fragile
He always knows how to make me smile
Having him was worth going the extra mile
We have a strong bond & tell me how he feels
Now that he's 20 years old, handsome & tall
He helps others from his heart & his free will
Others love him and for what he only reveals

I had Epilepsy for many years
I have a little miracle like no other
At a young age he was my home doctor
The day he was born I felt lucky to be his mother
Each passing years our bond gets stronger
Through his growing up he has grown mature
He was just 10 years old & he played soccer
His shirt number was 10 & a defense player
Too bad he only played one season that year

On the day he was born it felt so unreal
Having a precious baby boy with small hands
Ready to explore the world & see what's the deal
He is a very kindhearted young man & a friend
To see him blossom so precious & conceal
As a baby he was happy and easy to deal
As a child he loves kicking his soccer ball
I look at him & recall when he started to crawl
Today it's special because he turns 20 years old
He'll always be my Christmas Eve baby & my baby boy still
He was a bundle of love family always wanted to hold

I love him he's my whole life
He's the apple of my brown eyes
He's the best I can ever have
His eyes are two bright stars
He gives his love complete not just half.

HAPPY 20TH BIRTHDAY SON! I LOVE YOU!

"Discipline your son, and he will give you rest; he will delight to your heart."

-Proverbs 29:17

My Son Jesus

He was born on Christmas Eve & my Christmas baby
The day he was born he was the only premature baby boy
As a newborn family member never heard him cry
Every Christmas I have gotten him a real tree
He was one when he fell asleep by the lit-up Christmas tree
Growing up his favorite shows Arthur and Barney on T.V.
For Halloween he was a Hobo Clown, Black Ninja,
& Spider Man & Chucky
At seven months of July 26 he got his first teeth
As a toddler he liked to be being swigged from my knee
Through my years with Epilepsy he took care of me
While I was cooking, he always wanted to see
My son Jesus always stood and stands by me
I always told him to be whatever he wants to be
He always wanted to climb big and small trees
His favorite food is tostadas w/ beans, sour
cream, tomato, salt, and cheese
Likes to drink root beer and Arizona strawberry kiwi iced tea
He has continually been polite, nice, generous, sweet, caring, and funny
I told him the world I would want him to see
He likes his motorcycle, computer, music, swim, cell phone & MP3
His toddler & teen he was close to his cousin Jessica most of the time
As teens he would hangs out more with his cousin Stephanie
He's not much into video games but a lot into graffiti
He stands for what he believes in and his family.

"*Every good gift and every perfect gift are from above, coming down from the Father of lights with who there is no variation or shadow due to change.*"
-James 1:17

Now & Always Be My One & Only Baby Boy

January 12, got his first bath after 2 weeks
& his fallen umbilical I got to see
He loved the water in his baby bathtub I knew he will
-love the cool & salty sea
June 14, he was 6 months & his 1st visit to the
annually fair in Kings County
June 21 he was 6 months when he got on his first ride on a pony
June 30, he began to push the walker like a crab backwards it was funny
Father's Day of June 21 made his first trip to
the National Park of Yosemite
Our surprise we discovered he got his first teeth we were happy
July 27, he got his first baby pool sharing it with his daddy
August 15, he got baptized that day was full of harmony
September 27, his godparents invited us to Disneyland
-took a picture of us three
Four month later he took his 1st steps that was a special day
A day after his birthday we took him to his 1st to Sequoia
-National Park it was snowy
February 1994, we went to visit the zoo his favorite's
-reptiles & noisy monkeys

By the age of two years old he had four haircuts &
-a picture with his aunty Laurie
April 13 my parents took us two to Pismo Beach, CA on Easter Day
In November we went to Tepic, Nayarit, MX to meet his grandparents
In 1997 he was enrolled in kindergartner I was happy as a parent
June 2010 passed his DMV driving test this was one
-of his many accomplishments.

"But even now I know that whatever you ask from God will give you."

-John 11:22

Brother

Thanks to my mother I have
Two sisters and five brothers
No matter what I still love
Too bad we don't hang together

One of these silly brothers of mine
He became my role-model to me
I believe I use to do things like
I hold to these memories for my sake

He told me I can do anything
And be whatever I want to be
With his support our mother was ours
Friend & at the same time our father
He taught me how to use a bicycle & more

We played marbles & climbed on trees
He showed me to love our family
He was there for me & to love others
He never gave up on me even after

Having an illness called "Epilepsy"
Growing up by his side I looked high
To him & became my favorite brother

One of his T-shirts became my favorite
The one with Spud Mackenzie on it
Through my high school years, he made
Sure, I wasn't afraid awhile begin medicated
Him & my oldest brother toughed me
And to stand for myself & dry my eyes
Growing up with my siblings I was younger
Involved in their games and I was shorter

After a few stumbles in my life all there's
Small and manor bruises made by bad choices
Dealing being a teen & my unwanted illness

We became closer even though I played rough
Games I still used tennis shoes with pink shoelaces
Now that we are all older sometimes is tough
We all grew apart but always try to be near as

All I know having to grow up next to him
I was never confused in my heart having them
At times I wish we were all together once again

Like before at our home with our mother
In moments of heart-to-heart was a nice place
Our father left us young with our mother
My brother made me smile every year he's hilarious
Having to grow up with a humorous brother
Was like being up into space without medications
He has a warming smile just like our mother
His deep right dimple is like center of attention

Just like a child's mind suddenly wants
To dream and soar I close my eyes & he's
Asking me to iron creases on his shirt & pants
I see him clean cut & combing his hair back by
His light scent cologne always leaves
A positive image of his friendly & handsome face
He can be hard to live with like me but always
Tells you how he feels & sincere show he cares
Through our life journey we had our,
Differences I know he loves me his way
Growing up he was also my father figure
I would like to go back to those days any day
To relive those moments, I treasure
Years have passed us our hair became gray
He left his childhood behind & he matured
For my parents & siblings I always pray

I remember when he was into body building
Bought the wall stretching springs to tone
Up the arms and weights bench sitting
At the end doing curls listen to his tunes
On his boom-box by the window leaning
Against the screen he slept with it on
He still enjoys listening to his old school
Beats reliving those years were cool.

"A glad heart makes a cheerful face."

-Proverbs 15:13

December Child

Your *December* birthday flower
Holly plant meaning happiness
Respect & modesty from *Narcissus*
A friendship given faithfulness
Sign of the zodiac *Sagittarius*
Ethical, dynamic, generous
*Compassiona*te with others & humorous
Your birthstone is holy stone & *turquoise*
For good-luck charm & *priceless*
With Narcissus good & real *wishes*
Stay as sweet as you are *Chacha!*
It's believed that birthday celebration
Originated in the *Roman Empire* occasion
Origins of *birth* flower as the Narcissus
During Roman *birthday* celebration
Family and friends *offered* congratulations
Gifts like gemstone jewelry as turquoise
Origins of December birth flower Narcissus
Made history as the *first tradition*!

Hidden message of the birth flower
Victorian era varied *"You're the only one"*
White, orange & yellow colors of December flower
This flower is native to the Mediterranean
Region bloom under a cool weather
Embrace the meaning of your birthstone
With your flower with leaves erect & linear
Celebrate your birthday leaving a milestone
To look back each year before it disappears!

WE LOVE YOU BABY GIRL!

"God is within her she will not fall."

-Psalm 46.5

Just a Reminder

You are different from all of us the rest
Growing up to me you became the best
Life's mistakes you took them as a test
Of this life journey we all tend to reset
Try to leave life mistakes in our past
Treasuring good times in your chest
Growing up around you was total blast
Memories are better than resentment in the breast
Thanks for being there for me as my armrest
Under mother's eye we grew up to fast
Remember fly by mother's & visit her nest
Taking care of mother is our oath & a must
Take these words as a must or a small request
On your birthday I simply wish you the best!

No matter I will always end up I'll always love you
No matter what happens you'll always ne in my life
As kids when I was sad you always knew what to do
To bring & put a smile on my face like you always have
Remember the drawing I did for you for Mr. Carroll's class too!
Always love your first family & now your girls & wife

Another year to let you know you're older
Regardless our difference you're my brother
Growing up you were like my father
Thanks always sticking up for mother
You stand for what you believe because it's better
You never put me down with my seizures
Having you around me I felt less pressure
From schoolmates we grew closer
With your advices made me tolerant & stronger.

"Now there are varieties of gifts, but the same spirit."

-1 Corinthians

High Five

THUMB is considered the creative & insulator
INDEX finger is known as being outspoken
MIDDLE finger is more independent & cleverer
RING finger is known as a valuable token
PINKY's dream is to be a children's book author

As you can see the hand full is like no other
The only things common is the same mother
I got the privilege of seeing blossom like a flower
With different feelings but always together.

"I dedicated this short meaningful and worth mentioning words to a unique hand full that regardless how life may seem. They always seem to hold up together through the toughest storms as a teamwork. No matter how different they see life as they go with the flow or simply hard to live with each other. No one ever said life was easy we live, and we learn to appreciate. One another and the materialistic things it is offered to us."

Love Tia Lala

"Train up a child in the way he should go; even when he is old, he will not depart from it."

-Proverbs 22:6

Happy First Birthday

Today is your first birthday
A whole day full of fun & play
Seeing familiar faces of family
Consider today your lucky day
Congratulation on your 1st life journey
Your Great-great grand nana Cuca is not far away
Your birthday was celebrated on Saturday
On the sixteenth of 2011 of July
Enjoy your first birthday Party!
I know you can't read this today
But I know you'll read it someday.

Happy First Birthday Marley!

*"For through wisdom your days will be many,
and years will be added to your life."*

-Proverbs 9:11

Jessica Marie

No more playing with soft sand
Or play with washable finger paint
All those memories are left behind
Your most attention was my tea pot set

No more playing with dolls my dear
You became a responsible young lady
We recall memories of you and Jr.
Once you said you looked like me
You were always playing with iced water

You know what you want & one of a kind
You used to play with my baby doll
Nana Ocha always gave you & Jr. Kool-Aid
You were so natural thin and so small
Your hair was straight and your hands
Were so fragile your eyes were also small
As you smiled, they stretched like rubber band
We love you for being you most of all
You are loveable, caring and kind
I used love to see you crawl
Do you think you were spoiled?
You grew up to be thin and tall
Jr. & you were always holding hands
You would help him when he would fall
You were my only close niece I had

You would always be my first baby niece
You looked so cute the way you stood up
You and Jr. were a pair of mischievous dices
There was time you didn't like to clean-up
Your toddlers' memories are precious
You didn't mind sharing your zippy cup
Wish you the best in your journey in education
Or anything else with your cousin growing-up

You grew up so fast now you're in your
5th stage of life journey as a young adult
Most of the time you were in sports
Having you hang out was always pleasant
See you two spending time together
It was one of those special moments
They will stay within us forever.

"You are a Child of God..You are wonderfully made, dearly loved, and precious in His sight. Before God made you, he knew you..there is no one else like you!"

-Psalm 139

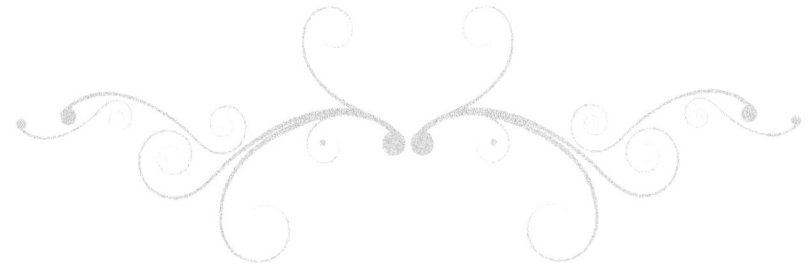

Inspirational

Blessing Friendship

I'm thankful to have you an inimitable friend
I know for the moment you're there & I'm here
I also know you'll be with me until the end
I know if you were around, you'll be right here
Thankful for your letters & warming respond
Thank you for caring & keeping me close & dear
Your friendship is special & you always go beyond
To let me know you'll me there for me & dry my tears
From the first day we meet we built a strong bond
Exchanging life experience & sharing our passion was clear
Enough for us those memories became close & fond
Deep in our hearts we became two secret keepers
I can honestly say "I love you" & watching the dawn
Just like embracing our friendship every year
We lost communication but I still gave you my hand
Our friendship is like a curious & playful kid and eager
To unfold the meaning of friendship that's until the end
No matter where life takes us, we would always be near
It's funny how we go through life & no one seems to understand
Us & we finally meet on a winter day you gave me your
Friendship like the wind passing through with a whisper and
Giving it so freely like the sight of the moon & the stars
Up above late at night you're the best I ever had
We have so much to give, share & places to explore
Especially you make me smile when I want to cry & sad
It's your love, respect; emotional support is like a sunflower

You are the sunshine of my purpose of life
Most of all the best I can ever, and I will have
Having you & be around me I never have enough
The times we were together we always laugh & have fun
Have long conversations every day or so on the phone
Was our way of our different point of view & opinions?
Of our different phases we all go through our whole life
I thank God for sending you to me and am the one
To give a new look in friendship & life like a new leaf.

"Greater love has no one than this that he lays down his life for his friends."
—John 15:13-15

Friendship Anniversary

It's been a year & four months since we meet
That is a date I will never ever forget
I will always treasure it with any regret
I hope I will never get you upset
Our friendship has no limits
Being with you is always pleasant
Hey friend, let us hold on tight!
To what we got and have built
Nothing & nobody can take us apart
We are close in mind & close in heart
The time I saw you I felt overwrought
You have never did me wrong or oversight
You got to know the real me & inside out
You looked where others would not
My poetries are my new reflect
So please keep me close to your heart
Every day and every night
Let's always remember our date
It's a date we can & will never forget
Even though I let you know early or late
Just to remind you the special day we met
Our yearning friendship is extant
I'm holding on strong and tight
To what we felt without any guilt
Let's live the past & treasure the present
Friend let's hold on tight
To our fondest memories
You're someone I can trust

Sweet moments are precious
A friend like you is pleasant
To have in my life is immense
Comfort & given with honest
Friendship and nevertheless
Giving me no space of doubt
Our moments are humorous
We each have what other doesn't
Bother to have in acquaintance
Love, respect, loyalty and *endurance*

That moment I knew I'll always be here for you.

"A man of many companions may come to ruin, but there is a friend who sticks closer than a brother."

—Proverb 18-24

GOD

God is internal life & good
Jesus is the hope & great
Without him I could not
Complete what's on my plate
Through my daily assignment
All my goals & accomplishments

God is love and happiness
Without his blessings
Most of all his forgiveness
God gave up his only son Jesus
Jesus shed holy blood
Until he was crucified
Nailed to the heavy cross
I always have trust
Upon him through my days
Of life here on earth

For my sins I make every day
I would simply be nothing
Every morning and night I say
"Thank you, God," for allowing
Me to see another of your glorious days
And for giving me your blessing

By enjoying the company of my,
Family and friends every day
To which is worth living
I thank you for giving me
Another chance in life
To help & take care of other's needs
By giving me the love
Guidance and strength
I'm happy with what I have
After all he placed us here on earth

Heavenly father you are my mentor
With your love & compassion
I don't dare to ask you for more
He made us in his image with devotion
He placed us here to help one another
All he asks is for some dedication
To him while being here.

"The Lord is my rock, & my fortress, and my deliverer; my God, my strength, in whom I will trust."

—Psalm 18:2

Good and Evil

You may look and smile similar like me
But you're not close to what people see
Because you can't love & care same as me
You are not the person you may seem to be
Because I'm unique & there's only one of me
You're a mad person & your trust is not guarantee
You are the bad fruit that came from a rotten tree
There can never be another of me or replace me
My love for others is different from the one you give
Instead of hurting others take my hand & come with me
And I will gladly show you exactly what I mean
With some help from up above you will feel his love
You like & know how to take away I like to show humanity
Your love hurts & my friendship is like a white dove
My way of showing some love is easy to agree
Life here is not about you and me to disagree
It's about peace & things to see what it's going to be
You charge for your friendship I like to give it for free
To love & respect others is the possibility of the main key
All you know is to disrespect and sting like a bee
I plant friendship seeds you sow & go on a hating spree
My love is warm yours is cold just like the deep blue sea
I speak with a normal tone you speak with an off low-key
I love the wildlife & life you like to watch others to die
I like to pass positive thoughts & you pass negative vibe
I open a door you're the locked door without a key
I bring happiness to faces & you bring sorrow and agony

My blooming flowers give pleasant scent yours attract plague
You give others your back I offer a leaning shoulder any day
You walk under a dark cloud I walk under a blue sky
With me I forgive, and you don't have any love or mercy
In an injury I take care of it & you break someone's knee
You want humanity to disappear I disagree! It should stay!
I obey while you persuade to play not know there's a prize to pay
I try to be realistic while you buy their souls & blind their eyes
Thanks to your greediness & evil forces in earth there's no peace
You can't take over my mind or stop me from who I want to be
You distract others from reality I try to bring them back by believing
I enjoy hearing others laugh you amuse yourself to hear others crying
I fight clean you like to fight cowardly with a double blade knife
I share sweet tea while you on the other hand give poisoned tea
At the end of our life journey we'll be where we should be our destiny.

"Be not overcome of evil but overcome evil with good."

-Romans 12:21

Reaching Out

It's my creative writing that helps me reach someone
Others reach out with music, gifts, greeting cards & me with poetry
In a form of a letter with meaningful words like a birthstone
It's like a musician creating rhythm into a special tone key
Like someone express themselves through paint like a rainbow
I guess it's natural to write feelings out that make others cry
That will show others the type of heart we have with a simple glow
It's nice to know & let other that comfort is only a call away
There is individual who are strong & others rather are alone
Staying away from interacting with others it's not good to see
You will be feeling lonely and picking habits that hurt slowly
Deep inside of those that care and loves you or will not deny
You to no one out in the street or when you're feeling blue
Because after all offering help & a helping hand is always free
It's a time to leave your pride & rancor aside don't be like a few
Who rather do things their way and say, *"my way or no way?"*
You may show you're of a strong attitude to show who's who
But in reality, the best tool to be successful it's to not runaway
From problems they show & the results is out of your reach too
It's better for your health to take whatever life gives you & enjoy
Whatever you accomplish to reach with the help given so true
It's a time of reaching your dreams and a new life journey
Because it's something we all tend to go through
As when we think all doors are locked and no key
To open it with a new attitude sees it as your cue
Those with a little extra help all dreams are worthy

Especially if you ask for help spiritually with a sow
Or simply start from scratch from A to Z
And you will see who you will be.
Don't do it for others to prove your point
But due to your power go with the flow
Your willing power & strengths are jointed
No matter how strong the wind blows
Don't give up in what you want
Stand strong & your confidence will grow
Reaching out is your cue & your check point
You will recover your determination slow
It will not make you any less confident
By reaching out to a helping hand & start to sow
We all need an extra boost when we just can't.

"It's yours, if you will but reach out your hand & grasp it."

Isa. 55:1 & Eze.36.26

Six Elements of Survival

God is the ruler of the universe
He gives us love and guidance
He has mercy upon & among us
His Holy Spirit is felt always
God takes us in his embrace
He brings faith, hope, love & peace
He holds our hands when we're confuse
Call upon his name to simply reduce
The burden you're carrying with a bruise
He will heal it slowly and place
You under his arm and foot trace
If you ever feel his spirit will show on your face
He created the earth for us to enjoy & our use

The **Sun** is one of our universe planets
In the winter it keeps us comfort & warm
Through the day it gives us light
Part of the world to the smallest worm
Just to feel the warm so radiant
Like the rays of the sun like a clear stream
To wake up with the sun is a blessing until night
It's always going to be a life giver & confirm
Useful energy fires like the sun we obtain heat
Upon his source of creation & our solar system
The fire alone it's a purifier, powerful & illuminated
In this world we all happen to share them
To continue & keep on loving we all depend upon it

The **Air** is our survival and ability to breath
Every minute of our appreciated daily life
From the moment we're on the womb to birth
Even the small bugs to the beautiful undersea reef
Are striving to stay alive with the air after birth
It's great to strive & live to the fullest in the wake life

To the ability to breathe every second is worth
To feel the wind caressing our face to the falling leaf Because
after all under God's eyes we're self-worth
Some of us we may or may not believe in after life
It doesn't matter as long your mind is down to earth
Each of us has our own strong & important beliefs
Air is feeling the freedom & our thoughts soar for us both
So, enjoy your life healthy and full of love good grief

The **water** represents the spiritual life force
Life to a new beginning and refreshment on summer
Water is important because we also use it as energy source
So, let's try to not to misuse the water & heal the future
Let's follow our common sense we wouldn't have any remorse
Of why we're running short on water while being here
As being part of this earth and let's enjoy the universe
These five elements of survival are our tools & life saver
If you think about it, you'll see what I mean on this verse

Earth works well with the air, fire, and the water
It's known they make the world go round as elements
It's proved to produce nutrients to fruits that are rare
As far we know the earth is the feminine component
It provides us with rich soil & clean oxygen to breath better
With the help of the trees, air current shifting & plants
She's fully of resistance, strength & been around forever
Green is for the grass, earth & for nutrimental soil to feed the roots
So, let's assist Mother Earth with what we can and be her helper
Earth is our second reason for our existence
matter in the world with test
Let us try to save the roaming wildlife & beautiful parks will disappear
She is more of a hidden & valuable treasure in a mysterious chest
So, let's embrace & cherish the moment in this natural element together
The only planetary that gives life & the third planet where the sun rests
As we all reduce unnecessary drive & walk short distance it's our share
And their functions that makes this planet earth & beauty of the forest
Earth embraces two colors blue for water & green for
plants & trees with scars

Earth happens to be the only planet that has living souls & see sunset
I let you decide for the reason of the humankind surrounded by water
After all it was created by evolution or just a celestial interest

Love is what makes this world go round and lovable
It is a deep emotional & affection we share with others
We all need love to feel alive & share its universal
Love can make you and others become much closer
With love & having it in your life you become untouchable
Love can bring you tears but heal your wounds each year
When you're loved it embraces you & feels comfortable
Love will give you happiness & sunshine like a sunflower
Love is like the genuine leather offering resistance & flexible
Love is felt for things, hobbies, pets, friends & lovers
Love is the second needed after God & favorable.

"Seeking the LORD and his strength; seek his presence continually."

-1 Chronicles 16:11 ESV/5

Special Prayer

God's love is so divine & good
It heals my daily life wounds

He loves us all & we're his best
To me he is forever great

Without him in my life
I can never or could be
Writing these words or alive
With him one day I'll be

His love makes me complete
Without his forgiveness
I'm nothing I appreciate
And accept his blessings

God is love and happiness
I plead you for my continuous
Sins everyday never less
He covers me with courageous
In the name of his son "Jesus"

I thank you morning & night
Thank you for giving me
Life and your breath so sweet
And see another glorious day
Giving me back my heartbeat
I embrace the company of those
I meet and love no matter
Where I am at every day & use
My manners to greet strangers
With a smile & a simple phrase
Thank you, Lord, for keeping me here

On this earth & it's worth living
Making memorial moments with family
Friends I call my own family tree

Walking in this unbalanced ground
Father I thank you for giving me
A wake-up sight keeping grounded
Granted me another life journey
Being able to hear every sound
Of my surrounding on my pathway

The Lord gives me strength
To be there and help others
In my time being here on earth
Heavenly Father you're my mentor
My forever light giving me faith
You give your freely love & compassion
To me in an old fashion & unique way
I never found in a simple emotion
Deep in my soul & braking chains away
As with me he made a new transformation
My lord & Jesus dry my salted tears away
You always answer to my petitions
Thank you for dying at the cross the day
You walked through this earth creation
Of my Heavenly Father for us to see

The beauty of this world and hold for us
To surviving in many ways and approval
Of you dear Lord, keep in your sweet embrace
Thank you for making my body movable
Keeping me safe and in your grace
With you in my life I'm untouchable
Please remove my burden from my face
You held me through things I was unable
To go brake barriers alone feeling confuse

It was your love for me written in a marble
Rock like the one you were thrown in your case
Many centuries ago, humans were horrible
Today you continue healing bruises
I learned your love is unconditional.

"Whatever things you ask when you pray, believe
that you receive them, and you
will have them."
—Mark 11:24

Yesterday is Gone

We are here gone tomorrow
Let's love one another
It's a time to let others know
Whatever happens to you I care
And old we shall all grow
You don't know me but you're dear
Life is valuable & we can't bear
Of losing someone we deeply know
So, let's say; "I love you" while being here
Let's take the advantage now
Before walking out the front door
Feel proud for your good deed & take a bow
Because tomorrow may not be here
Gone forever like the sunset view
It's a time to dry our eyes & salty tears
Let's see every day like a new rainbow
Dare to help others that others don't dare
After all every day we get what we sow
So, go ahead give a smile with a friendly stare
Or you can even smile and say hello
All because today it will fade away & disappear
Yesterday is gone and no longer glow
And now to be realistic laughter
It's a great medicine that works slow
You will see sharing a smile is a lifesaver
Enjoy your day no matter how

Life may cut you deep & leave a scar
And how strong the wind blow
You will see life is not a burned-out cigar
Treasure the people around you
Bring them together in a simple prayer
So, don't live your life like a scare crow
Take pleasure in things you do for others
Yesterday is gone like hiding behind a shadow
After all, under God's eyes we are all brother & sisters
Yesterday doesn't have to feel like death row
See it as a moment to think about it and be aware
Of our actions passing by us like a slide show
Instead allow yourself to feel like a shimmering star
There's nothing like recovering from a gut blow
Yesterday is like life either good or fair
After the day is gone our eyes are close like the dawn.

"His anger endures but a moment; weeping may endure for a night, but joy cometh in the morning."

-Psalm 30:5

Gone for A Moment

I was here and gone for a moment
It has been seven years ago

I walked and walked towards a shimmery light
Without any guidance of a flashlight

I kept walking in the misty white thick fog
I approached it with the hope to see the light
Behind the thick, white wall of misty fog

I was experiencing a feeling I didn't understand
While this phenomenal switching was occurring
I do recall still being in the hospital bed

From a corner in the recovery
Room I was mental recording

Listening to the commotion going around
From a small corner I see my dead body laying
I see and hear medical staff shouting out loud
"Bring the Respiratory Therapy Machine! She's not responding!"
Physically I was there; spiritually I was up in the clouds

The eerie part about this I didn't feel lonely
It was like entering into a different place time zone
The entrance was foggy and heavenly
It was My Father welcoming me from his throne

After seeing a luminosity smoke rise up
From my dead body with glow and slowly
I can still see and hear the cardiac monitor sound
Going from normal to low hearing it clearly
I hear saying "clear!" one shock "clear" two shocks
and open my eyes gradually
I hear the electricity of the "shock paddle" while being below
I was brought back from the "dying heart pulse" very slightly

At that moment I remember opening my eyes lightly
and seeing the ceiling I asked myself," but how?"
I can honesty tell you it was astonishing and felt harmonically
Coming back to reality the first word I hear was "hello"
I recall this strong real-life event yearly
I suddenly felt my body being shock high and fall back slow
Through this experience it taught me life is freely
Not reaching to the gleam light I knew it was not my time to go

Few hours after being back through resuscitation
I realized life is precious family and friends
I take in my heart and consideration
Because they are mine forever until the end
After all I am one of his many breathtaking creations

Subsequent, to dying for two minutes this poem is just a translation
Our Heavenly father's love for us has no limitation
I felt his tender lasting loving care and his affection
He gave me guidance through the fog and gave me his protection
Therefore, I glorify his name through this documentation
This is just my small token and a valuable notion
At that point I become conscious of my reasons
Of breathing and his proposition
With these unique lines of words is my small demonstration
For what he has done and still doing for me
Every day I show appreciation
Ever since my life after death experience my
Life took a new transformation
Now it's been eight vivid breathing

Years & I still don't ask him any questions
By believing, trusting, and having faith
Upon him are his qualifications
Be content with what we sow and have
He listens when I have a heavy emotion
Our Father gives us his infinity love
In many ways and forms of communication

There is no human power that can bring us peace & salvation
Like our Heavenly Father's unconditional compassion.

"The Lord is my light and my salvation; whom shall I fear shall I be afraid?"

—Psalm 27:1

Motivation

Motivation can start by having a simple conversation
Keep in mind the sky above you have no limitation
As, long you have the mind, heart, and passion

You're a mysterious treasure box and
You hold the magic key of dedication
Don't allow others stop you from your hand
To fulfill your dreams & ambition

Remember you are the key holder
To your own life destination
You are always your own driver

Keep the mind & soul towards ambition
The one thing that makes the difference
In life is called focus with determination
Leaving milestone in your life experiences

There's no such thing as having enough of education
The unique about the mind it's by your way of manipulation
Through our lives we make many unsure delegations
At the end of your hardship you will get through any situation
Maintain your full energy and eagerness on conservation
Every journey you set has its worth compensations

Self-talk and hanging out with supportive
Group is a positive communication
Once reaching to the top of your goal with strive
You'll be overwhelming with emotion
Negative comments are just made to have attention
The hardest thing to do it's the idea of making a new inception
Focusing & staying on top of your priorities
Nothing will break your concentration
Reach to someone you trust & is supportive
Going forward with your aspiration

Checking yourself doesn't mean
You're running in a competition
Keep your head on your shoulders
Don't let others take away your reputation.

"Wait and trust the LORD. Don't be upset when others het rich or when someone else's plans succeed."

—Psalm 37:7

Be Yourself

Be who you are and always be true
For the real person that you are & do
Be whoever you want to be & start to sow
Don't do what others want you to do let it go
Be honest to yourself & let other know
Of the person you are & how others feel about you
Do what you want to do for yourself don't get sold-off
Remember that temptation life doesn't last long
Only you have control of the lifestyle & it will show
Do things for yourself not for others to just throw
Try to live a normal life don't fall & live on the low
Stay away from little troubles it may take you to death row
Be a positive image & role model to those who look up to you
Because not only the love for others but the respect will grow
It's always nice to walk out in the streets & hear others say hello
Prevent to fall into a gap in life that could be hard to undo
If you're walking against a strong wind dwelling you
Down you will get through it because you're not alone
Don't take being alive & the ability of your whole
Body movements for granted be well-known
So, go ahead put a smile on a child that feels alone
Or on another person that's been blown

Away & a person that has an
Upside down smile as frown
Be yourself act silly be a social
Butterfly even acts like a clown
Continue to be supportive even
A protector or someone's backbone
Be proud of who you are and be
A true friend & love your birthstone
Feel good about who you are head to toe
Allow others see your heart is not made of stone
Scream, jump, skip, chill, or get-up-and-go
Be modest, humble, close, outspoken, cheerful, or sad & blue
Demonstrate yourself that you can also be happy with a glow
But whatever your mood maybe I'm sure it will be shown
Live life to the fullest & live it healthy leaving a milestone

Advice: *"Don't do anything that may hurt yourself or anyone"*
Sleep late or be an early bird, be respectful, share your love
Because you're always going to be the owner of your throne
Be a close friend a secret keeper or a leaning shoulder on the telephone
But let me remind you don't do this only because I say so.

"Create in me a clear heart O' God. Renew a right spirit within me."

—Psalm 51:10

Love

"Love letter"

(November 26, 1989)

"Hello Stranger",

"As I sit here" "thinking of you". Now that you're "always on my mind" and that it's you that I care for "always and forever". "I'll make it easy" for you if this is hard for you to understand it. "Heaven must have sent you" to me so we can be "Sincerely" the "best of friends." If not, I'll ask you "Why can't we be friends?" If you ever need someone to talk to "Just look over your shoulders" and "I'll be there."

For you on the good and for the bad times please remember "you got a friend." So "I'd like to get to know you" better. And knowing that you're "1000 miles away" every night I'm "wishing upon a star" lying down on my bed writing you this special letter. And thinking to say, "please Mr. Postman", (to the mailman) make sure that my sweetheart receives this letter because, "It's sealed with a kiss". Sometimes I feel as if we were "distance lovers" because, right now you're miles away from me. I always get a "happy feeling" whenever I receive your phone calls or those warm letters you send me with sweet words. It makes me feel like "A special kind of love" we share.

You will always be in a special place in my little heart. So, "you'll always be someone special" to me. I hope "It's okay" with you sweetheart. I hope you "remember me" sometimes because I always remember I always remember you. One day I was "sitting in the park" having one of my day's "dreams" of "you and me." And before it fades away I told you "I'll always be there" for you on sunny and rainy days. "I'm so happy" that I met you by a friend. Because, if it wouldn't be that we met by her I wouldn't never had this special relationship with you.

"Thanks for being a friend" at the beginning of our friendship we built from day one when, "your eyes met mine." First, we were two strangers then friends and then "lovers never say good-bye." After I snapped out of it,

I realized that it was *"just a dream"* of mine with you. Even though this was just a daydream of mine *"being with you"*. I want you to keep this letter. And only God know how much *"I love you"* and *"I miss you"*. So, take care and God Bless you always.

    "Sincerely" yours, Claudia Walthing

Tommy

I still remember the day we meet
It has been him that I can't forget
Summer season was over & we grew apart
Oh, I can't forget his face so sweet
Nobody knows when I'm hurt
Inside with an aching heart
Profound thoughts day and night
Feelings arise deep in my heart
To which I cannot take apart

I cannot respond or love any body
With my million pieces broken heart
Unless it's the love of my life Tommy
That has come back and never apart
He will always be close and near me
He will end my burden broken heart
I know each year he would ask about me
In summer season he's in my thoughts
People knew I'm the one he always loves

It has been twenty-two years
He's been deep inside my heart
He's been within me all these years
Ever since then I have been hurt
I've been holding on to his name
His memories I cannot take apart
I know I have not been the same
I hope on day I will not regret
In playing my own mind game

I loved him so I have his initial
Tattooed on my finger as his signal.

Destiny

Destiny is just a mysterious fate
I still remember when we first meet
To the place we went on our first date
We shared a feeling that we didn't hesitated
Through our looks and our touch, we demonstrate
Our true sentiment & to us we know what they meant
Suddenly years went by & we didn't communicate
Once again, our eyes met but by then it was too late
I had a baby boy & had someone to serve his plate
After our lives took a turn on us, we didn't participate
But our roads got crossed & old ashes started to create
Later on, down in life because you are my future & my past
I recall you told me with a golden rose ring you love me the best
You introduced your little girl to me & to my son she got attracted
Being around & face to face neither one of us knew how to act
At that moment all I learn by heart seeing us four happy and content
The funny thing about our destiny how we felt it was no secret
Our love was from a distance & with a smiled we only associate
Years pasted by & with our new partners we got separated
To see and hear about you was something I couldn't wait
Time went by not knowing anything about you I got frustrated
Through my relationships I don't seem to find my mate
I don't know why it's been so long & it's you I can't forget
There's been time all I want it's to run & flee to ventilate

Because of this passion I have no control but then yet
Our special kind of love was like no other silhouette
The day we had to say good-bye was a hard moment
I can still and feel my salted tears as if it was recent
My resentment is I wasn't strong to go against
My highly and authority for respect I cried out silent
In moments I look back at those love messages you sent
Deep in my heart I believe once again we will have contact
God knows where you maybe at mile across from the start
Even though you will never be apart from my heart
So, until then I shall carry this burden heartache
You are not just another love you are important
I pray to the heavens to keep you safe sweetheart
I blame the love cupid for aiming you and me as its target
They all know how I feel about you is not a hidden secret
Its' your memories that's keeping me alive and complete
I still believe if destiny placed you in front of me in the past
When it does, I will stand for our love & always be content.

Sunday

We meet on a cool Sunday
And in a very casual way
Since then its' a special day
I never thought of you think of me that way
After that there was nothing that kept us away
We were having a good time that we wanted to stay
I know we'll see each other one day not faraway
That's the first time I heard the word, Orale!
I was once asked if I believed in destiny
To me it's like a uncover mystery

Just like this insignificant poem
This line runs through my
Body like a peaceful stream
It's something you uncover for me
Having to meet you that day was like a dream
I felt we were going to be close from the start
If I can, I will give you my heart
Thanks to you my poetries in my life took a big part
They become my most valuable piece of arts

I once was told I was not like other girls
That day I knew I was not just a spring fling
You exposed your love for writing songs & your singing
That day I knew I was walking into an odyssey
We have talked about our heartstrings
It was your smile and personality that was charming
With a hug & hand shake we said good-bye that evening.

It Was You

You taught me the meaning of holding on to love
To value it defend it was something totally new
It was a feeling that grew & it was granted to have
You are always next to me when I'm gloomy and blue
Our love is honest & pure just like the beautiful white dove
Having you next to me I always feel safe & brand new
All because you became to be my knight & a huge part of
My present life & for the rest of our life it's just us two
With you everything is I can ever have and dream of
This day on you & me belong together like the morning dew
Together our bodies dance to our rhyme so unique groove
It was the love arrow that belong to the cupid we both knew
I believe you got sent to me by God from the heavens up above
You uncover my deepest emotion I had out away & decided to do
It was you who I have been waiting for all through my lonely life
Your honesty caring & your love help me get through
At the end of our life journey I don't see you there I will prove
Me to you that it was you who I love all my life & I was into
You because I was the one whom I love the most and pickoff
All those men out there waiting and searching for a clue
To pick it up and embrace it even when life seem tough
Together I know we can pull through & continue to pursue
Happiness until the end of our remaining years of proof
Of love between two is hard & full of devotion to which few
Don't know how to survive without one another & speak of
It was you who me be a believer once again in love of two
They are willing to share everything with one another in love
Your love brings me harmony in mind like calmest meadow
I learned there's a time if we love someone, we must let it go
Because the love I receive it's giving for free & sometimes it's sow.

Thinking of You

I've been thinking of you
It gives me an excited feeling
Just by the thought of you
Simply to know we have been talking
To constantly writing & thinking, too
You can count on me any seasonal day
Thinking about you with happiness
24/7 from Monday to Sunday
It's my way of you & our closeness

Here I am thinking when we first meet
I took you as a stranger and meant
I accepted you as a mutual friend
Days turned into a beautiful sunset
I hope that our friendship will never end

Before I knew days turned into weeks
My feelings became stronger in the weekends
I was tempted to give you a kiss on the cheeks
Like the light of sunshine when it peeks

The weeks turned into a month
You came into my life in a casual way
Your friendship is true & will not be stealth
We meet a month ago & started to talk freely
Now I don't know what to do with a breath
You are a good person to hang out someday
Amigo when I don't hear from you
My mind cannot think straight
The thought of what you're going through
It hurts me to accept the fact that I can't
Be by your side we're few miles apart, too
The start of a strong friendship & respect

We should not have to hide though
You are always close to my heart
Because I got the pleasure meeting you
No matter how many miles we're apart
I know your honest friendship is true
It's your personality that captured me from the start
Here I am thinking of you, why? I don't have a clue
Ever since then we try to stay in contact
These feelings to me are new
All I can say I'm glad I'm thinking of you.

Honey Kisses

I love you before I met you
Your kisses are sweeter than sugar
It was in a beautiful dream so true
Your kisses are like no other chocolate bar
Your lips touch mine like the morning dew
With your kisses I can reach the stars
Wave to the moon & see the comets too
I got to see the galaxy & the shooting stars
Your kisses are like out of this world & new
It's like walking on air holding me with care
Nothing matters in this world only us two
I know that our dream is not that far
To become reality with a kiss in the clue
To see you next to me like the ray of the solar
With your sugary kiss my sky is clear & blue
It's your sweetness that makes me want more
In the dream it was your lips that drew
Me to dream away and set my heart to soar
Me to a deep transient as if it was past due
Your sweet kisses can't be bought in any store
Because it was meant for me to take it into
My body and keep it with me forever

I embrace the touch of your lips that you blow
Those kisses only for me like two flirtatious lovers
Your love & your sweet kiss is something that grew
With a look & a touch I got to experience that power
The sweetness of your kiss that made me reacts to
Your kiss like beauty of the mysterious ocean floor
It was your engaging kiss that drove me to your love
Our love & the sweetness of your kiss is like a flower
That brings spring blossom & the pureness of a dove
You woke the deepest of my heart & ready to explore
A feeling that only two can come together like glue
A kiss is a question that only you have an answer
To a sweet kiss like honey from your lips so true
The taste of your sweet lips contains such a unique power
So natural like the harmony sound coming from the meadow
With the taste of your kiss takes me to the highest tower
I will stand by your side no matter how strong the wind blows
Because your honey kisses are the envy of many others
For the first time in my life it was luck I got to know you
Now and forever my life will be sweet every precious hour.

Today and Always

Today, tomorrow, and always
As I don't see you my days are blue and gray
For you & your family I always pray
We should meet again and catch up at a café
Let's once again get together on a Sunday
What do you say? Órale
I will have you within me
It's with you who I want to be
You are the one with the master key
Being with you it's like going
On an adventurous shopping spree
Our names are carved in
The trunk of the oak tree
Moments together our feelings flow free
To keep in touch, we did agree
Not thinking about you it's not as easy
I like to see your name on my caller I.D.
Our thoughts are like a water stream
Flowing in harmony with me
You will never feel lonely

No matter how much it hurts
I will never get tired of sending
You occasional greeting card
You held my hand that night in
Front of your house front yard
We share about the same memories
Of childhood growing up background

My poetries are my guard's feelings and
You're my shinning knight with his sword
At that very moment we meet
My feelings kept moving forward
Our conversations are a valuable reward
Not thinking of you is going to be hard
You're in a special place in my thoughts
Writing about you I think I broke
My many & deep writing record
You're too deep inside my mind
Also, too deep in my loving heart

What we have going on is strong
Our bond is an unbreakable bond

You'll always be like a spot of gold
Hard to keep and hard
To keep a strong hold
This relationship is so devoted
Something we continue to unfold

We will always hold on to our,
Feelings even after we're old
The place we came from
Summertime is very hot
Today and always my
Feelings for you can't be bought
I trust you with my open eyes
Or having my eyes blind folded
Of what we felt and built let's
Have a very strong hold
We have built a solid
Friendship undoable knot

Our walk at the close by park
Is for today & always
Just like the good size duck pond
Rain drops of love was falling
Will be our favorite spot
The best part about
I can't stop thinking about it.

Us

I live in a city known for the Tachi Palace in Lemoore
You live at a commercial city call Bakersfield
Our feelings have never felt so sure
For the moment feeling a little wretched
I just want to know about you more
We are only a few miles apart
My family knows your family from before
But always close in mind and heart
I recall the day you stood by me by the door
It was great that we got together and interact
You proved to me your friendship & love is puree
This is not just a fairy tale of us it's true fact
Before visiting your family was our sincere
The day I meet you made a strong impact
We both have talent being two writers
Using expressive words on a paper as shield
It's cool that we all share sense of humor
Over time our friendship has been a battlefield
Our families shared childhood stories we shared lore
Within a year of our close friendship it was intact
Your uncle played his well-known guitar
You did a duet with him & sang to my mother
Favorite song she just loves and adores
Our conversations many were heart-to-heart
Funny how we became close friends & afraid
Of the outcome what we felt was something more

Days, weeks, months went by and we kept
We did our best in keep up with our contact
It's a yearning feeling for what
Both of us & our hearts couldn't ignore
Never made a deal or singed a friendship contract
The day we meet neither of us was aware
Of what it was going to unfold like a pact
You say, "Was it, coincidence or destiny?"
For not going to the concert that night
With our conversation I became lively
Our family's acquaintance was pleasant

I was glad to know you did not
Made it to see Zapp's concert I would
Never meet you to make eye contact
For the first time I made a real friend
Knowing you from a childhood was a start
In you I found a friend until the end.

Volcanic Love

I been loving you
All my years existing life
My love & feelings for you
I will love you until I die
Feelings have grown strong
Each moment I'm convinced
You leave ashes behind along
The times you stop coming around
You burst my heart long ago
Full of flaky ashes as ground
Feelings that still now fulfills me
With passion as a true-life
The day you stop loving me
You cut my heart with a knife
Years are passing quickly by
Us like a fugitive like a thief
You stole my one and only
Seven days a week & 9-5
It's your sweet love I carry
In my veins like hot lava flow
Leaving a scar behind already
Like a crest in the earth long ago
Your devotion is a system that feels good
Very majestic hard to let it go
It motives to go look forward
Gets me ready to always strive and
It's your love that made an opening

In my heart showing a glowing rainbow
Your sparks of love make me
Loveable & gives me a unique glow
Your showering love gives me energy
After all it's your magnetism & volcanic
Love it's what's keeping me alive
After I leave this world your volcanic
Love will be a scar even after life
Leaving the best memories & fantastic
Sparkling fire in ashes I like to have
Like they say where there once fire
There's ashes & it can sudden grow
Embracing the love before it disappears
Making its way with an overflow
Allowing your heart to a new explore
Grounds hard for me to let it go
Your kind of affection can drive
Anyone to the edge of a cliff
Is something I would like to live
Left behind on the ground as a relief
Showing me to turn something negative
Into positive & start to just believe
In a true love that's always positive
Like high temperature of a volcano
It's forever no one can ever undo
Of how I feel about you is real
I don't think & believe of how I feel

Is hurting or doing anyone wrong
Willing to love you with a strong will
Your love is like a new solid creation
Marking a new beginning of evolution
Just like lave that flows down the burping
Volcano to underneath of the reefs
Giving my life an ending & a new beginning
Pausing the world for a moment of grief
Your name is an ever more love tattoo
That's imprinted on the tip of my tongue
So, leave my heart burst in fire like pyro
Of deep passion burning all year long

The mentioning of your name
Sparkling stars appear on my handkerchief
Ultimately, I have been wearing on my sleeve
Your heart & mine together make a fine
Music notes as duets in a love song
This volcanic love is driving me insane
Feel full of energy & forever young
It's real not just a make believes
Shall live within us & forever flow.

You're Gone Again

Here I am back in my loneliness
I'm sad and lonely because
I don't see you I miss our talks
And our ways of closeness
I haven't heard or seen you
You have me so confuse
Since May & now it's June
My broken heart I'm giving it to you
In my hand & along with my emptiness
That runs deep in my heart and in my soul
You've gone again without telling adios
I feel as if I'm sitting in the back of the row
I thought we had everything in a working progress
You're gone again and all I can say, "Wow!"
Out of all my close friends you
Were the most propitious
Since you've been gone my
Heart became a weeping willow
After we found each
Other I was full of happiness
Just letting you know
I need my friend now
Since you've been gone
I'm here alone with sadness
I must find and know
About you somehow

Ever since you've been gone
My mind has been a mess
If you don't want to be
Around just let me know
After all I'm just another homo sapiens
With a heart ache I will have no
Other choice but let you go
All I know is that my feelings are on the loose
All because our conversation at
First was high & now it's low
Whenever you decide to come back
I will be here waiting here I guess
Meantime I'll be sharing my tears with my pillow
Since you have been gone all I hear is bits of intermezzo
I believe you went through this same repeated scenario
I'm afraid that by now my heart has become spacious
Filled with questions and papers saying no show
Inside the space in my heart there's a small box
You can't deny that our need for each other is matchless
At the beginning our friendship was a beautiful
Flower that the wind would blow
Regardless how hard the wind would
Blow they will still be the best of friends
Because the wind knows that he brings
Out her true colors in a fashionably glow

That's his way of giving her his soft touch & warm caress
Having the wind blowing on her petals that make her grow
Until one day the wind she enjoyed a lot stopped jocose
He stopped swinging by her spot all she hears is his "Hello!"
Days went by just like the flower missing the wind
And me missing you we both became morose
The wind and you are the one to blame because
You two left us & took our spirito
Though you're gone again you can never be replaced
No matter how many storms I have to go though
You will never be my careless nemesis
After all I just go with the hard & bumpy flow
It was you who stood out more that
Any other book in a rare bookcase
Though it's been 2 years & 10 months
It feels as if I knew you from long-ago
At the same time as you, being, gone
Away I was drowning my heart in a wineglass
Why didn't you tell me you were going again?
Was it too difficult for you to tell me so?
All I've been waiting for you by the hourglass
In ran into many people but none are
The same as you are in being simpatico
Being without & not knowing about you
It's like being in a dark maze

I will keep on holding on to your memories
And writer's advices if it's the very ultimo
Thing I have and keep of you I will bury it deep
At the bottom of my heart & treasure box
Every Sunday that comes & goes I feel closer to
What you left behind along with your shadow
Along with your birth sign as a Water Bearer
Playful, fixed waters and a true Aquarius
Just like you are being gone and you
Being a true Aquarius, it really does show
And with a red and yellow dark rose
Is to let you know somehow
This is my way to have this letter closed.

School

Coach

A coach is like the Golden Eagle
It prepares you for what's ahead of you
Just by giving you a look and signal
A coach is the best person you
Will and can ever know

A coach will train you in a heartbeat
Will guide you with awareness
As, long as you have what it
Takes and no one can take it apart
Their wisdom & technicalities they posses
A coach will teach you what
He knows from the start
They will work hard with you
Up on and beyond your progress

To which it will make you strong
They will be haughty of whom you become
During a lecture of courage words
He wants you to keep your headstrong
Listening to him your heart will beat like a drum
The mind and body are set to soar
And do your best at every game
A coach is a great educator
He wants you to feel the urge on the chest
Take the coach's advices seriously

That's their way to show consideration
Taken a deep breath you will become courageous
A coach should have some type of recognition
For the fact few may not come through for us
Its' always nice to talk to a coach with no hesitation
Throughout life we rarely meet excellent coaches
They're very few those that we show appreciation
To have a coach & athlete relationship is priceless
Not very many will show their emotion

Some may carry and have a serious look
But under that look they are not so fierce
A skillful coach can read you like book
A coach will take you under his wing
He will start training your way to hook
Your body, spirit, mind and opening
Your eyes to everything you need to know.

Eagle Hill

Eagle Hill is not just for any eagle
But for the one & only from West Hills
And known as the Golden Eagle
I may be gone but you will be here still
Your spirit will be caught in the middle
It all started from the best of Laton Hill
The coaches push our strong will a little
You gave me courage & not easy to be kill
In the competitions & still run with style
Completing in a good place it's not a big deal
I've been planning to tell you for a while
All the hard training I saw it as a drill
To be the one to embrace it & still smile
You gave me wings on my shoes going uphill
While for others you are just a dirt pile
Miss having sand in my tennis shoes going downhill
You give natural energy that felt so unreal
It's your spontaneous feeling that gave thrill
Every time I ran & crossed every mile
You crossed my mind when I hear the bird calls
Running or stretching on the riverbed was real
That allowed my imagination to feel & fulfill
My needs of focus that made me feel like steel
Leaving behind unprinted and unique trail
Like the main source of the leg is the muscle
No one will ever know how much peace you reveal
That is why I embrace those moments so memorable

To feel the weight as running on the soft sand
It's a feeling not everyone is able to understand

Your powerful wings help prepared me to soar
To high sea level to the low of the valley floor
To my home the well-known town Lemoore
Where I was proudly raised and unnatural born
It was you who gave me strengths and more
To accomplish my goal to earn the highest score
To stay healthy & active in sports you open a new door
Every challenging running course & testing my body motor
By going back to you & having sandy shoes I didn't ignore
Being able to reach the top of the hill was a good view for sure
Training on the cold and soft sand was like being on a tour
At the end of mental training I loved the feeling sore
Afterwards, I would feel with more energy than before

The smell of the wilderness in the morning dew
The cool air enjoying the moment of what I like to do
Hearing and embracing Mother Nature when I run
Feeling the morning light on my face the warmth of the sun
Sharing the team bonding and the coaches' push was fun
But as for me training season are never gone

It's like a farmer's responsibility in his farm is never done
That's why Eagle Hill in Laton is my favorite & number one
It was the environment that helped me do the long runs
I took that experience and it became my main back bone
Like my biggest event in my life the first marathon
By gaining the experience to be closer to earth like a stone
The full understanding of training with you it's engraved in stone
Like those memories we built together like a milestone
Your natural growth & the beauty you conceal is my flagstone
From a distance you can hear a dog playing with his bone
The busy farmer working on his earthy ground is no comparison

Hearing the engine of his tractor is like listening our heart
The land keeps him alive with providing for his family
Like our hearts keeps us alive and from the start
From the first we see and bond in a place where we can be
Free and get closer with our inner self and be apart
From our normal lives & close to the wonders earth energy
And take something in that no one can ever replicate
Like the roots of our generations & the grass around the tree.

Educator

Thank you for being a noteworthy instructor
Not only a fine teacher but a worth mentioning teacher
Thank you for being an excellent listener
Thanks to you my way of thinking is more mature
I recall years back you gave me a hand as a starter
You're doing something that others don't do or dare
Your way of teaching shows you really care for others
You helped me plan my goals and just learn more
It was you who taught me to be a fast thinker and be clever
Thanks to your push to try something new I became my peer's leader
As years pass by as you will always be close and very dear
You took me in your class & stood by me from January-December
Through your red pen marks & critics you taught me to be a fighter
Never give up on the first try just keep trying
to do my best & study harder
As a student and an athlete & now just an explorer
To a dedicated & respectful competitor
I learned from your visual examples to your
Hands on learning and your informative lectures
You taught me the ABC's, stay healthy, fractions, life science
The meaning of history to become a continuously a writer
Thanks to you I can see myself having a successful future
You facilitated me to gain more
Knowledge & prepared me to soar & explore
Just like West Hills College, Lemoore motto
"Once you go here, you can go anywhere"

It was you who encourage me to move forward
Thank you for believing in me I earned a few awards
Through my levels of education, I learned that mind
It is a powerful tool even when things look hard
As I made new approaches you stood by me like a lifeguard
You followed me through my childhood to my adulthood
You gave me your hand when others wouldn't & couldn't

You taught me well to learn from my first mistake & never give up!
You're the one who help me get through my stage of education
You taught me I'm in charge of my own destination
You're the one who answered me as I had a simple question
It was you who knew and help me discovered my true potential
Thanks to you, education is notorious all around the nation
My hat goes off to all of you who give education a true definition
It is every single of you who gave me a chance & motivation
Thank goodness for the excellent education foundation

You help me pull through every moment such as frustration
Because of your push and patience, I got to
Experience the true meaning of graduation
I see all of you with a tremendous respect and admiration
In receiving some type of completion such as a certificate
Major degree or a diploma is our compensation
You help me break many barriers & contentment
With a student & teacher conversation
It is the educators that introduce and train the new generation

I also believe it was our one on one
Clarification & our communication
My return to college was a totally college
Experience & unexpected expectation
You are the one who helps us open our mind
& use our developmental imagination
All of you make a beautiful and
Colorful bouquet of flowers that contain
Such as forget-me-not of good memories, freesia
For the full spirit, fern for confidence
Ivy for friendship, static for victory
And success, pink tulip for caring
The pink carnation for gratitude and iris for inspiration
Each of you in one or another made us
Realize to make realistic and be caution
Of our goals that will take our life to a new transformation
Please accepted this humble poetry
As a small token of appreciation
To those educators who guide me
Through school participation
I dedicate this meaningful poetry
As you're devoted and to education.

I dedicate this poem to my *Island Union School, P.W Engvall, Lemoore Union High School & West Hills Community College, Lemoore* Chancellor, Board of Trustees, Administrators, Athlete Department, Career Center Technician, Librarians, Counselors, Athlete Counselors, DSPS counselors, Staff: Disable Student Program Services (DSPS) Lab, Coaches and Clubs Advisors.

Garden of Friends

It is said true friends is made of seeds to makes a beautiful garden
It's where ivy is for lasting friendship full of magic with fern
Each year our friendship was held strong & beautiful like a cabin
It was filled with trust & full of spirit from freesia and fine
Yellow roses for joy & friendship I will never
forget you with pink carnation

I give you red roses for love and respect along with daisy for loyalty
We all had sincerity and strength of character coming from gladioli
We came from different background & we
grew up together like a family
As children we all played different games but wild and free
As we got older our life took different life pathway
But our true colors and spirit was full of glow & beauty
Our inner self grew with burst like a butterfly
Like our way we chose our adult life journey
At the end of our life turn is see later not a good-bye
So, let's live to the fullest and meet up someday

In my garden different backgrounds and pleasant flowers such as:
Sunflower, sweet peas, pink tulip, variegated tulip, blue violet
Magenta zinnia, mixed zinnia, yellow zinnia, forever ivy, pink roses
Ivy, larkspur, full of palm leaves, peony I have met
And kept close to my heart along with nasturtium, primrose, iris
General rosebuds, yellow, dark pink & red roses a lot of respect
Beautiful flowers and rare like snowdrops, caladium & freesias
They offer geranium for comfort, caladium with joy & delight
Red chrysanthemum willing to share & general flower so cheerfulness
With many pleasant of good memories of forget-me-not.

Lemoore Tigers

Feel the strength and hear the Lemoore Tiger's roar
Be proud of having the opportunity to attend Lemoore High
Because you have captured the majestic spirit of the tiger
Yes, we were wild and free but never did we ignore a simple "hi"
Golden memories for life are friends we make in our freshman years
It's an unforgettable experience it can easily pass you by
So, go ahead wear the purple and gold with pride and honor
Because after all the two colors combined are powerful and so fly
Thanks for extra push of the counselors & helping hands of the teachers
My most memories are the punk and gangster style with a look so classy
Who can ever forget the colorful bandanas
& dual colors of the leg warmers?
Head hair nets, bright and dark colors, the
feathered hair style & hairspray
Old school jams on cruising nights in stylish low-rider cars
Downtown Hanford on 7th Street and Visalia on the street of Mooney
Stylish derbies, Kaki's to Soot Suits & parachute pants
introduced by MC Hammer
Black & bright color wrist bands to Teen Angel and Hot Rods Magazines
We were the new generation and the bright future with royal power
Popular artists Kenny Logan, Guns & Roses, Michael Jackson, and Blonde
The Go-Go's, Berry White, Pat Benatar, Prince &
The Revolution & Cyndi Lauper
"Up town girl", "I miss you", "Material Girl", "Eye
of the Tiger" & "When dove cry",
"Friends", We are the world, "Every breath you
take" & "Living under the prayer"

Popular movies Teen Wolf, Gremlins, Fame, Karate Kid
and Rocky Balboa "Rocky"
Notorious cartoons Strawberry Shortcake, Smurfs,
Thunder Cats, and Care Bares
As for T.V. shows Mace, Punky Brewster,
Who's the boss, and Happy Days
I'm sure we all remember Elm Street movies and Night Stalker
Last minute crave before class running to Wayne's Market for an iced tea
Years coming and going by us while our bond
stay's strong and still together
Regardless where life takes us you shall always remain inside of me
Lemoore Union High School is forever it will
be our old-time sake's keeper
Just like the well-known Video Zone and The Arrow Stationery
Domino's Pizza and the new kid in town Mc Donald's came to Lemoore
State Competition for Mascots gained and brings the victory
Best ice cream in town Superior Dairy and Thrift's Store
I still carry your purple and gold tiger paws imprinted every day
Next to my beating heart and it will remain as a tattoo on me forever
We were very devoted students to you from Monday through Friday
Vacations and weekends came between,
but we went back for some more
Thanks to your support and encouragements
we experienced graduation day
You watched over us through our freshman,
sophomore, junior and senior

Year you taught us to be a fighter a true warrior and these rules we always
obey
All we leave behind is our prints & our four years with you
now it's time for us to explore
You gave me knowledge of a leader and to
be an example to our community
I leave my roaming school spirit along with my echoing
conversations and laughter
I know one day we will see each other and
our happy faces not that faraway
So, until then allow me to treasure and cherish those happy years.

Purple and Gold

Embrace the power of purple with royalty
Lemoore Tigers is the one with spiritual riches
Those who attended can feel the power with loyalty
Empower the yellow gold with deep significance
Four years of school were dedicated with dignity
To be part of the purple & gold brings kindness
Gold is notorious for emotional and prosperity
Purple is known for its wisdom and mysterious
Gold gives you inner growth & personal maturity
The feeling is once in a lifetime & memories so precious
Like the strength of the purple gives me spirituality
My mind, free soul and spirit you got to nourish
There's nothing like having the pride of a Tiger Lily

Through school we gave ourselves with devotion
With gold let's hold close to success & true friendship
By adopting the purple you'll gain self-knowledge
Along with compassion for others & sportsmanship
Combining purple, gold & a tiger you'll have courage
That wraps you with its beautiful colors and strips
Their majestic eyes so intriguing and so strange
We were wild and free like a young loving hip
The color of Lemoore Tigers grows with our age
It will welcome you as you take the hardest step
On your first day of class and ready to change
From a young teenager to mature adult with a tip

You will never regret in your preparedness for collage
Because the classy purple & gold offers scholarship
For your future and goals before walking the stage
With honor and fulfillment upon your survivorship
Passing the Lemoore High School student's gauge
Take in as much knowledge along with the tips.
Our tiger spirit gives us insight & prepares us to soar
To introduce ourselves to nature with a historical roar
With your purple and gold coach us to go & explore
Full of dreams and adventures through the year
The unique colors taught us to be a true warrior
Thanks to the will & patience of devoted counselors
Along with the courage & wisdom of a distinctive tiger
To empower its strength & spirit it will stay in you forever
Feeding from your true soul and lead you like a mentor
The tiger spirit will guide you from freshman to senior year.
"Go Lemoore Tiger! Feel our spirit with a roar!"

Island & P.W.E Friends

It's a keep sake keeper reflection
A valuable sight through an hourglass
We all enjoyed class discussion & participation
We became like family every year's class
We shared special moments before detention
We confessed many secrets sitting on the grass
We all were there for a strong education
It's the grade school memories we can't let it pass
Through both schools I made many friends to mention
In school it didn't matter where you came from mid-class
We were all the new future wild & free generation
Through our elementary & junior high we had our 1st crush
Of what we have become there's no space for duplication
My Island School Third grade favorite teacher was Mrs. Alves
We built a lasting friendship bridge a strong foundation
We can't forget 8th grade teacher "My Friend" Mr. Ross
I believe there's no broken bond with our way of communication
From the first time I met all of you in my heart I keep you close
To my Island & P.W.E. friends I give you this with dedication
Because after all this special poem is real and all about us
Every time we see each other is worth the celebration
Our years of growing up we had a few stumbles & bruises
I can really say all of you have become my inspiration
You and your real friendship bond I hope never lose
Every year in my heart you created a garden of carnations

Each of us remember something of a favorite teacher
We watched & cheered many games from the bleacher
There were moments together we cried sad & happy tears
You stood by my side all those times and school years
Of our strong friendship love to others we made it clear
We all continue to keep in touch now that we are older
I thank God and you too helped me as I had a seizure
You never saw or treated me any different from others
I will never forget the All Class Reunion the day we got together!

The Golden Eagle

Hold ourselves to the highest standards of sportsmanship
We demonstrate our strong performance and characteristic of bravery
From this point on everything is all about teamwork and friendship
We are the protectors of our West Hills College territory
In Golf, Soccer, Cross-Country, wrestling we go through hardship
But is all worth it because; we leave it as part of hereditary

We are proud to be a faithful Golden Eagle
We take pride in our West Hills College
And what it means to be a true Golden Eagle
Honor and uphold the traditions of sports knowledge

Appreciate the privilege of wearing our Navy and Gold
Embrace the unique perspective each of us bring to West Hills College
These two colors are powerful to be proud of and to hold
Support our fellow student-athletes in their pursuit of courage
Together as a team we are not so easy to hold
We all get the same courtesy and open privilege

The Golden Eagle is known to be the King of all birds
Navy and Gold at a competition we became courageous
At the end of our season all we leave behind is our proudly prints
In being a Golden Eagle is all about school spirit and confidence
From today on we will always carry Navy and Gold colors
Be positive role models for our families, community, and college
West Hills College, Lemoore campus is our pride grounds

We are the exemplary and we compete with honor
All we leave to our full of pride "Hall and Fame"
In addition to our respectful coaches who are our mentors
We leave behind our Golden Eagle spirit and our name
Once you become a Golden Eagle your heart will soar
Looking forward to another season and improve each game

We represent the one and only West Hills College, Lemoore
I give these few words to the Athlete Director and its' administrators
I will never forget my two years as a Cross-Country runner
Learning from my teammate and coaches my mentors
Thank you all of you for my college experience as a runner.

Purple Heart

He was a man like no other
I meet him back in Junior high
He was my eighth-grade teacher
He always gave a warming "hi"
"Hello, my friend!" was his greeter
To all students with a high five
He gave us years of advices & laughter's
I showed him he was appreciated when he was alive
As a human being he was the finest coach & teacher
A coach who pushed you to your abilities & strength
As a teacher he never gave up on his students every year
His smile gave positive attitude & always to strive
He told me always believe in myself and soar
High for my dreams just like anyone would have
Young & old him for me he was a fine polisher
He was willing to help you see yourself and prove
Yourself of your hidden strengths you hide from peers
Slowly he would unfold part of you until you stood tall & brave
Through new classes materials with his supportive without fear
You faced every educational year full of eager & full of life
After 8th grade he reviewed my grades through high school year
With his unique way of teaching he feed positive words the mind craved
To learn more & the ears to hear more to me he will always be dear

He was a strong man like a Grizzly bear
But he had courage and a big heart of a lion in land
Through the life he held together with an invisible tear
Yearly he covered his deep & painful wounds
With his warm smile & positive attitude ready to hear
Anyone who was willing to challenge themselves & would
Want to learn & grow as an individual & explore the power
Of the great will power we tend to use & we could
Easily be wasted away and covered full of fear

Not letting the wings of our hearts experience the word "proud"
As a unique & essential educator always gave me comfort with a cheer
I was able to open-up with my fears & he was one I trust and
Someone to confine in with my teen trouble through my younger
Years through Junior High School & experiencing the young adult hood
He was someone trustworthy with conversation
between student & teacher
He gave examples & coherent of lectures for us to understood
This magnificent dedicated teacher opened the doors to a better future
I did never saw him worried or frustrated had a great smile that had
The energy he gave with his enthusiasm &
professionalism like a true soldier
In my life he became an inspiration & a rare
milestone legacy that was good
He and his wife are always dear and close to my heart & prayers.

"I dedicate this poem to a devoted educationalist, coach, and most of all a respectable a confidential friend for life! Miss you and love you Mr. Ross! You may be gone to heaven to continue your notorious teaching, but you have never been forgotten here on land. You like others gave a new meaning of Education. Thank you and you will continuously stay within along with your one on one talks about how to strive and never give up my dreams and goals in life . . ."

Island Elementary School

1979-1980 Third Grade, Island Union School, Lemoore
Mr. Bates was our school Superintendent for years
You welcomed me friendly I wanted to learn more
It was your warm smiles that gave me tremendous valor
To continue to practice my English and new sky to soar
With your support I became my parent's interpreter
Knowing I didn't speak English you & I played on the tower
Every recess we played and being watched by a duty teacher
With you I learned my first English words & I got better
For four years in good ol' Island School we had class together
To different classroom activities & coloring with color markers
To my favorite poem "The Lark" in a textbook of literature
Friends I made down my way each year more than before
In Mrs. Alves classroom she had a pet tarantula there
Eating roasted peanuts, red and black liquorish & good behavior
It was one of our treats after a good spelling word test score
Through the day she would scold us but to me she was dear
Mrs. Fonts was nice and sweet Teacher's Assistance & fair
She would invite me to her house to bake homemade sugar
Cookies, chocolate chip cookies and sometimes peanut better
She introduced me to her husband and her only daughter
Her house office desk would be with piles of folders & paper
She drunk a lot of coffee and a caring—loving mother
Who can ever forget fourth grade teacher Mr. Shaver
Seeing driving into the school's parking lot on his VW car
Tall and slim man wearing wide eyeglasses & with little hair

Had a deep voice that as a kid you didn't dared to just stare
You had to look into his big eyes and speak clear
1981-1982 Mrs. Brown was a nice Fifth Grade teacher
In her classroom there were eighteen students being teenagers
Full of life and each year we would bloom like a sunflower
I still recall Mrs. Ross who was approachable & her helper
Thanks to Mrs. Fonts & Mrs. Ross I became a fast learner
Mrs. Louis Ross wore thick and big eyeglasses and coffee lover
They worked with Spanish speaking students for those unsure
In reading small work in class the Migrant Program Educator
Always was there for our improvement to understand better

1982-1983 Sixth Grade Mr. Fraley was a great professor
He was straight and forward sports coach and a schoolteacher
Not only that but he was someone who was cool & sincere
Therefore, I wrote this poem about you it was time to explore
With you I gave my first step now I am back stronger than ever
You gave me a truly clear vision of my education & my future.

My First Friends

Island School 1979-1980 Third Grade:
Cindy was shy and light brown hair
Always sweet like a sweet pea flower
Al Lee always athlete & cheerful
With a personality so unique & beautiful
Nicki has soft voice & always sweet
That's like a geranium that gives comfort
Elizabeth always smiling with limitation
She is full of gratitude like a pink carnation
Shawn blood sister was a kid's game
Since then our sister love has been the same
We were both on a quest like the nasturtium
Natal always sharing her warming smile
Like Cleopatra the Queen of the Great Nile
Nicole full of dreams an always shy
She has a happy life so healing like a peony
Mary had a serious look & young hearted
Third grader with a big heart and a friend
Anthony her twin brother had nice wavy hair
He hardly spoke and just ready to soar
Bill so giggly & so mischievous
Joey has a I didn't do it smile
He always walked with the group in a file
Michael was shy as he would talk
He had a witty attitude and a unique walk
Greg was a character with golden hair
Friendly smile & flirtatious dark blue eyes

Through the school year they became close & dear
Good old memories are worth gold & I embrace
Reuben was a very well-kept young man
He carries himself simple & was tall & slender
In school we all had dreams we played & ran
We lived out in the country wild & free to explore

Bobby was slender with very wavy hair
He was like a jewel that's unique and very rare
Ted very energetic & not easy to dare
Great personality warm & caring like a Teddy Bear.

Island School 1981-1982 Fifth Grade:
Evan always spoke clear and so sweet
In sports he was light on his feet
To have him around was a cool treat
Josephina was a very humorous friend
I will take her and the others in my heart until the end
John had the most shinny golden healthy hair
His personality was a bit shy but so friendly
Too bad he didn't have a choice to complete that year
At the end of fifth grade year he moved away
Tina shows her love in her caring best way
Like a sunflower brings sunshine & friendship of ivy
Just like a anybody we had dreams & took a pathway
Ramona & Jesus were brother and sister
In class they were smart and blossoming like a flower

Anthony has a delightful smile and look
Through the years he always had an opened book
Michael so friendly and so sweet but shy
I give them all a yellow rose for our friendship & joy

Island School 1982-1983 Sixth Grade:
Tami carries herself so beautifully & a warm smile
Having her as a friend her number all I had to just dial
John an easy going and cheerful young man
We all lived out in the country where there were big barns
Chris was about my size but a good friend
Being around him, I was me there was no need to pretend
Just like every single of them they do cross my mind
Kari is a very tall and slender not to mention energetic
She had reddish hair it reminded me of Strawberry Shortcake
Robert had the most warming smile and eyes
He was tall and slender I'm sure he was good in basketball

In the school yard and classroom, we all had our space
After all these pasted years I haven't forgotten them at all
Rebecca her bright smile gave me comfort & trust
Her petite size and beautiful eyes gave a vibe of honest
Dina a very cheerful young hearted girl
Big eyes and so natural wavy hair smiley and slender
I am sure she was great in sports such in the hurdles
She was a very pleasant and likeable sixth grader
Josephina was a very caring and positive
She lived by the river and there was a big oak tree
Jimmy was an excited young man in school
He had a very eager attitude but always kept his cool.

*"Just like each of them they stayed in my healthy heart.
Wherever our life journey takes us I will never forget
those valuable and golden school memories apart.
From deep of my heart to my deepest thoughts."*

www.ingramcontent.com/pod-product-compliance
Ingram Content Group UK Ltd.
Pitfield, Milton Keynes, MK11 3LW, UK
UKHW022224230426
12048UKWH00016BA/1049